IMAGES
of America

CAMP RILEA

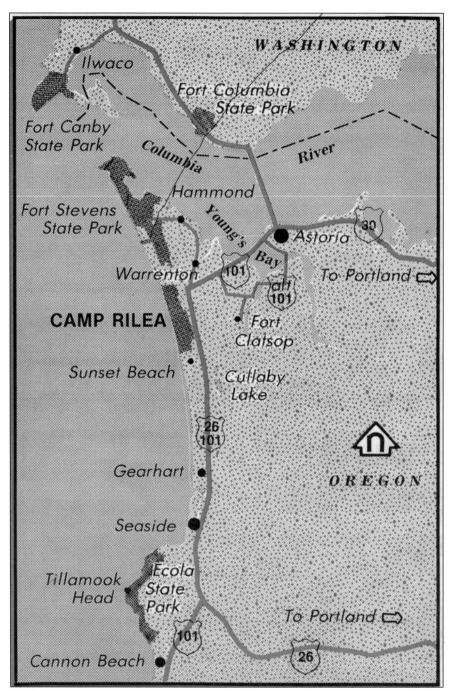

Camp Rilea is located on the northern Oregon coast, in close proximity to several communities, historical points of interest, and outdoor recreation. (Courtesy of Oregon Military Department.)

ON THE COVER: Company M, Eugene, guidon flying, marches into Camp Clatsop on a newly installed dirt road for the 1927 inaugural encampment after detraining at the Clatsop train depot. (Courtesy of Clatsop County Historical Society.)

IMAGES
of America

CAMP RILEA

Andrea Larson Perez

ARCADIA
PUBLISHING

Published by Arcadia Publishing
Charleston, South Carolina

Printed in the United States of America

Library of Congress Control Number: 2014934892

For all general information, please contact Arcadia Publishing:
Telephone 843-853-2070
Fax 843-853-0044
E-mail sales@arcadiapublishing.com
For customer service and orders:
Toll-Free 1-888-313-2665

Visit us on the Internet at www.arcadiapublishing.com

*Dedicated to all who have passed through the gates of
Camp Rilea in service to our nation and to the citizens
of the surrounding communities for their support.*

CONTENTS

ACKNOWLEDGMENTS

Many individuals and organizations require acknowledgement for their generosity, support, assistance, and expertise in completion of this book about Camp Rilea: Ronald D. Kinsley, Warren W. Aney, Lt. Col. Alisha Hamel, Mike Williams, James "Jim" Miller, Lt. Col. Shaun Martin, 1st. Sgt. Jeff Dintleman, Maj. Robert Wagner, Liisa Penner, Gary Henley, Alex Pajunas, Laura Sellers, Lori Tobias, the staff of Camp Rilea, Oregon Military Department, the *Daily Astorian*, Clatsop County Historical Society, and the Camp Rilea Archives, to which I was given unfettered access. As a first-time author, I would like to thank Rebecca Coffey, acquisitions editor at Arcadia Publishing, for her support and guidance on this project, and Susan L. Glen, Arcadia author and genealogist extraordinaire, for her assistance in getting this project off the ground.

I am happy to have the opportunity to thank my family for their enthusiastic support of this project, of course, but also for their service to our nation. I am not a veteran or a military historian. I am the daughter of a veteran, the wife of a veteran, and the mother of an active-duty soldier. After three decades writing for others in advertising and public relations, the irony of my first book being on a military subject is not lost on me. However, events in recent years have stirred the patriotism within me. As a member of the Daughters of the American Revolution, I have developed a deep pride and understanding of my 12 (or more) generations of truly American ancestors who have helped define, defend, and protect the freedom I enjoy on a daily basis.

It is through this lens that I approached this book about Camp Rilea. I hope readers come away with an appreciation for the history of the post and a better understanding of the important training that occurs there and the dedication of those who serve our state and nation as part of the Oregon National Guard.

Unless otherwise noted, all images appear courtesy of the Oregon Military Department.

INTRODUCTION

In recent decades, Camp Rilea was nicknamed the "Jewel of the Pacific," indicating the high regard for its many offerings and attributes within military circles and for the many and various organizations served on the post. Fewer and fewer people, however, remain to tell the story of this important military training site that officially became Camp Clatsop on March 1, 1927. Not intended to be the definitive history of Camp Rilea, this book attempts to enlighten readers about its history, evolution, and current and future roles through the photographs on the following pages.

As early as 1907, Oregon's north coast between Astoria and Seaside was favored for National Guard training. Sites throughout the state, like Camp Jackson near Medford, were also utilized until the high transportation costs and distant locations became an issue for soldiers and military budgets alike. After a comprehensive statewide survey by the Oregon Military Department, Camp Clatsop was chosen as a permanent site. The site was ideal for its many desirable features: its proximity to population centers, its nearness to Fort Stevens, reliable rail transportation, and excellent water supply. The mild climate and varied terrain also offered training opportunities for troops from across the state and region.

The site was to be known as Camp Clatsop. At the time, the name seemed like a good idea, due to the camp's proximity to nearby Fort Clatsop, a popular landmark and, more than 120 years before, the winter quarters of the Army's Capt. Meriwether Lewis and Capt. William Clark during their expedition to find the Northwest Passage. This decision would soon be the subject of debate, due to ongoing confusion of tourists and military trainees attempting to find either Camp Clatsop or Fort Clatsop and frequently ending up at the wrong location.

Originally, the land comprising Camp Clatsop Military Reservation totaled only 363.5 acres and was leased in 1927 from landowners by the Astoria Chamber of Commerce for $2,253.50 per year. Over time, the Astoria Chamber of Commerce looked to the Oregon Military Department to take over the lease and then exercise its option to buy the property for $39,225, a term of the original 10-year lease. As a result of action by the 1929 Oregon Legislature, the lease was taken over by the State of Oregon.

Once the State of Oregon took over the lease, the size of the site was increased to 413.5 acres in March 1932. While the term of the lease was still in effect, there were constant calls for the state to purchase the site, allowing for the possibility for additional federal dollars to flow into Camp Clatsop for the installation of permanent facilities instead of the annual tent encampments that were the norm for the time. Until that point, improvements to Camp Clatsop were paid for by state funds.

It only took a year for the legislature to appropriate $30,000 for the purchase of Camp Clatsop, and on November 3, 1933, the purchase of 548.5 acres was approved at a cost of $25,511.05. As anticipated, many permanent improvements were made to Camp Clatsop throughout the 1930s, which allowed the post to become the best training facility of its kind.

With the onset of World War II, Pres. Franklin Roosevelt mobilized most of the Oregon Guardsmen by executive order in August 1940. By 1942, over 6,000 men from the Oregon National Guard and guard reserves entered federal service. Most of these soldiers came through Camp Rilea on their way to war.

The US Army continued to use the base throughout the war as an extension of nearby Fort Stevens. A variety of army units used it as a training and staging base. In 1948, Camp Clatsop hosted the first post–World War II encampment of the newly reorganized Oregon Army National Guard. Camp Clatsop easily reestablished itself as the primary training site for the Oregon Army National Guard, supporting the needs of the military during the Korean War and continuing readiness for any domestic contingencies.

Since Camp Clatsop's beginnings, Maj. Gen. Thomas E. Rilea had been integrally involved in its existence. He commanded many, if not most, of the annual encampments taking place on the post. Serving as Oregon's adjutant general from 1941 until his death, Rilea had a keen interest in the post during his storied career in the Oregon National Guard. Immediately following his death in 1959, Camp Clatsop was fittingly renamed Camp Rilea. More of his pivotal role in the history of the Oregon National Guard is covered in the chapter dedicated to him.

After a brief period of declining use at Camp Rilea, its superintendent, Brig. Gen. Richard McCarter, took over in 1973. He brought new interest to Camp Rilea as an annual training site for the National Guard and other units of the military. By 1975, the camp was partly revitalized for use by a variety of military units, not just the Oregon Army National Guard.

Always a continual process, the focused energy in the 1970s set the stage for a major expansion of Camp Rilea's facilities and roles beginning in the 1980s. Under the leadership of Oregon's adjutant general at the time, Brig. Gen. Raymond F. "Fred" Rees, Camp Rilea was reestablished as a premier training site for a variety of modern military needs. It developed modern troop housing, state-of-the-art firing ranges, and many specialized training sites. Working closely with facilities manager (and longtime friend) Ronald D. Kinsley, this leadership team brought its vision of the future into being at Camp Rilea.

In the 21st century, emphasizing an environmentally sound approach, Camp Rilea supports infantry squad training, airborne and amphibious training, operations in urban areas, Special Forces and Ranger training, combat engineer training, leadership training, and training for peacekeeping operations. In order to support those expanded offerings, the Oregon Military Department leased over 350,000 acres of nearby forest land from private timber firms and the Oregon Department of Forestry for use by units up to brigade strength (about 4,000 soldiers). This adjacent training area consists of rugged mountains with several summits exceeding 3,000 feet, rolling hills, and low-lying floodplains. Units from other states and countries also train at Camp Rilea, including Canada and Great Britain.

As the permanent home of the 116th Air Control Squadron and the 234th Engineers, Camp Rilea is also a popular site for hosting civilian, school, and professional activities, events, and programs. These include national track events, Naval Sea Cadet training, soccer meets, school tour groups, football, wrestling and band camps, and historical reenactments. Camp Rilea has also become an important training site for federal, state, county, and municipal law enforcement agencies. Beginning in 1998, Camp Rilea was designated one of three Theater Specific Individual Readiness Training Sites (TSIRT) for National Guard, US Army Reserve, and regular Army units being sent overseas.

Many may be surprised to learn that today's Camp Rilea is comprised of 1,800 acres and employs a full-time force of nearly 120 personnel. Annually, over 125,000 users enter the gates, generating $8–$11 million in the economy of the surrounding community. Indeed, there is much to learn about what happens "behind the dune" at Camp Rilea.

As the mission states, "Camp Rilea supports the Oregon National Guard to provide the citizens of the State of Oregon and the United States with a ready force of citizen soldiers and airmen, equipped and trained to respond to any contingency, natural or man-made. When we are needed, we are there."

One

THE EARLY DAYS

The first encampment of the Camp Clatsop era began on June 15–29, 1927. Headlines in local newspapers heralded the arrival of over 3,000 troops to the area. Brig. Gen. George A. White, Oregon's adjutant general, and his staff were in command of this inaugural encampment. A large crowd has gathered to witness the annual "Grand Review." Note the company guidons proudly displayed on the ridge.

This, the oldest known image of Camp Clatsop, shows initial construction at the front gate of what is still the main road into the post. Local contractors Charles Noe Rohaut and Edgar G. Gearhart were hired for the job. Preliminary surveying prior to construction work was done by G.T. McClean, an Astoria engineer. General White and other dignitaries attended the ground-breaking ceremonies for Camp Clatsop.

A.B. Gerding worked with John Slotte and Company to construct the road from Roosevelt Highway (now Highway 101) to the center of camp. Since troops were scheduled to arrive soon after June 1, 1927, the construction firm was offered $10 extra per day for early completion. The road was finished on May 13, 1927, resulting in a $176 bonus. Here, guards from Astoria's Company L are posted at the entrance of Camp Clatsop on that dirt road.

As the troops arrived at Camp Clatsop each year for their annual encampments, they became familiar with this view of the front gate. Thousands marched on foot with heavy packs from the train depot, and truck convoys carried the necessary equipment, food, horses, and more troops through the coastal towns to their destination for training.

The main road is still not paved in this photograph showing the evolution of the front gate at Camp Clatsop in the early days. One by one, new buildings appeared. Guardhouses are visible in the foreground, the quartermaster building is to the left, and the gymnasium is to the right.

Many of the troops and supplies arrived via the Lewis & Clark Railroad at the Clatsop depot on Roosevelt Highway (now Highway 101). While most of the soldiers marched in formation to Camp Clatsop from the depot, trucks for transport of equipment and troops stood ready. The Lewis & Clark Railroad was part of the Spokane, Portland & Seattle Railway (SP&S).

In the Clatsop County Historical Society's Fall 1989 issue of *Cumtux*, it was made clear that the Lewis & Clark Railroad played a significant national security role well before it was used to transport troops to Camp Clatsop for training from around the region. About 1918, the highly prized and locally available Sitka spruce was needed to build "aeroplanes." This led to the building of the Spruce Line (later called the Lewis & Clark Railroad) off the SP&S, with a stop at Camp Clatsop.

Detraining of the troops at the Camp Clatsop depot was accomplished smoothly, with trains arriving in 15-to-30-minute intervals throughout the day. In addition to the many trains that thundered through Astoria bound for Camp Clatsop, there were several special cars of regular infantry from Vancouver Barracks. These men acted as the "training instructors" for the encampment.

Because interest was so great in the summer encampments at Camp Clatsop, special train service was organized and promoted for those who wished to witness the annual event. The round-trip fare from Portland was $3, and the schedule allowed for travelers to have dinner in Astoria prior to the return trip. The service ran daily for the duration of the camp.

Camp Clatsop, Ore.

Shown here is the arrival of several companies of troops. Marching through the front gate (background, left) on the newly cleared and graded road, not yet paved, they move past the quartermaster building (right) that still stands today, with the same overhang profile. Often, 20 counties and 30 different cities and towns were represented among the many units in attendance at annual encampments. (Courtesy of the Clatsop County Historical Society.)

Thousands of automobiles visited the annual encampments. Parking was an issue at all times of day, even along the Roosevelt Highway, and many cautions were issued by state traffic officers for drivers and pedestrians. Once off the highway, the motorist turned into Camp Clatsop and a courteous sentry would direct them to the parking area. Picking up walking Guardsmen along the highway was encouraged, as many of the troops walked to activities off-post. The men greatly appreciated the lifts.

Company M, 186th Infantry, from Eugene, Oregon, proudly arrives at Camp Clatsop for its two-week encampment after detraining. The original company guidon, seen here, can be viewed at the Clatsop County Historical Society. (Courtesy of the Clatsop County Historical Society.)

"Visitors Always Welcome" was the refrain from the camp commander and adjutant general of Oregon, Brig. Gen. George A. White. The message was spread to encourage attendance at events held during the encampments. Civilians were welcome on-post, daily, until 10:00 p.m. Returning the sentiment, the surrounding communities enthusiastically welcomed the troops to the area for their training. Astoria and Seaside hosted special events, including dances, parades, and meals hosted by civic organizations.

After arriving at camp, there was no time to spare. Each unit marched to its designated area and immediately pitched shelter tents to establish itself at camp and prepared for the training to begin. Most of the images in this chapter show favorable coastal weather for these activities. It is easy to imagine how rain and wind would change every aspect of training.

Once the tents were pitched, troops focused on what was called the "shake down" inspection. Each man laid out his personal equipment according to regulation. The precise instructions for this display were followed to such a degree that only two or three minor infractions were reported at the 1927 encampment.

Under the eagle eyes of the commanding general and his aides, inspection at Camp Clatsop was a serious and detailed endeavor. In one report, an unfortunate soldier was missing one pair of wool socks, which, he explained, had disappeared. With the exception of such minor deficiencies, every man was found to "be ready for field service. Arms and military equipment were declared complete, modern and in condition for efficient use," according to Brig. Gen. George A. White.

In this detail from a panorama photograph, the early sand road into the center of Camp Clatsop runs left to right. It appears that the arrival has concluded, tents have been pitched, and the group has been successfully installed at Camp Clatsop.

For the first time, all of the units of the Oregon National Guard were able to train at Camp Clatsop, as it had the space, facilities, and varied terrain to accommodate their needs. Indeed, the concentration of troops at the annual encampments at Camp Clatsop in the early days exceeded the numbers of those during World War I. In this photograph, the great expanse of the Clatsop

Plain accommodates the large number of canvas tents housing over 3,000 men. This panoramic photograph was taken by Frank W. Woodfield. Born in Astoria, Oregon, in 1879, Woodfield documented many aspects of life on the Oregon coast for decades. This original photograph was purchased at a local garage sale for $5 and given to Camp Rilea as a gift.

After the successful 1927 encampment, effective lobbying directed funding to Camp Clatsop for a target range, additional bathhouses, and latrines designed to serve a battalion. Over the years, further appropriations allowed for additional buildings, including a camp hospital, and an electrical power system. By 1939, the evolution of the tents to house troops was complete. Walls had been added to the tent floors, making living conditions much more hospitable.

In 1931, P.L. Read, a Portland contractor, was the lowest bidder to erect 14 mess halls and two officer's bathhouses. The work of tearing out the old buildings was overseen by general contractor A.W. Quist. All of the work was contracted to be complete by June for the next summer encampment. Many more permanent structures are visible in this photograph from the late 1930s.

In October 1930, Maj. Gen. George A. White announced more new construction, an increase in allotment of federal funds to Oregon, and a total in excess of $230,000 to be spent on training and camp for that year. By the late 1930s, Camp Clatsop was rated the finest training site of its kind in the country. This distinction helped fuel the expansion and the economic impact Camp Clatsop had on supportive coastal communities.

Here, troops are involved in daily activities at camp. Horses played an important role in these daily activities. Not limited to the parade field, they were corralled at Camp Clatsop and used frequently to move heavy equipment.

Every company unit had many training goals while at camp. The diversity of the terrain at Camp Clatsop presented excellent "classroom" opportunities for simulating battle scenarios. However, small-group instruction did take place in more traditional settings, as shown here. The quartermaster building is visible at left in this photograph, taken around 1935.

Maj. Gen. George A. White reported 2,947 officers and men in attendance at Camp Clatsop as of June 17, 1927. The number was expected to rise above 3,000 within days. That number was more than the commanding general estimated in his pre-encampment report; 700 more than the War Department expected; and a full 1,000 more than at the previous encampment, held near Medford, Oregon.

In 1938, all officers in camp at Camp Clatsop and Fort Stevens were received by Maj. Gen. A.H. Blanding at the commanding general's base at Camp Clatsop. Major General Blanding, chief, National Guard Bureau in Washington, DC, and Maj. Gen. Albert J. Bowley, commander of the IX Corps area, joined General Rilea for inspections at camp. In departing, Blanding complimented the fine camp and the state of troop training.

After a "microscopic" inspection of the 82nd Brigade and its attached units conducted by Major General White and inspectors from the regular Army on the fourth day of the encampment, it was determined that, "should the United States need the services of the Oregon National Guard to protect the nation from invasion by an aggressive foe," it would be ready and fully equipped to do so.

Upon his arrival at Camp Clatsop with a special escort, Gov. Charles H. Martin was greeted with a 17-gun salute. The Grand Review included all of the field equipment, the quartermaster's convoy of 160 trucks, the 186th Infantry Band, and all units in attendance, totaling over 3,600 troops. Here, the honor guard of the 186th Infantry leads the parade on the last day of the 1938 encampment.

Here, the company guidons (flags) are on full display during the "Pass in Review." Some artillerymen were worried about the depletion of ammunition supplies leading into the battle demonstrations due to the number of generals and dignitaries at camp requiring salutes. The first time the entire Oregon National Guard had trained within the confines of a single camp was in 1938, under the command of Brig. Gen. Thomas E. Rilea.

Pass in Review on horseback was an integral part of the ceremonies at each encampment. In 1938, a crowd numbering in the thousands lined the Spectators Ridge to witness 12 of the 155-millimeter howitzers of the 218th Field Artillery being rolled into position in the natural amphitheater at Camp Clatsop. The big guns were set for their demonstration just after the 3,600 soldiers marched past in the annual Grand Review.

This photograph shows an in-ranks review by Maj. Gen. George White and Oregon governor Charles H. Martin, who served in the US Army. A West Point graduate and veteran of the Spanish-American War and World War I, Martin retired and served in Oregon politics, including one term as governor (1935–1939).

Paying the Oregon National Guard his first official visit, Maj. Gen. Albert H. Blanding (standing, third from right), chief of the National Guard Bureau in Washington, DC, arrived at Camp Clatsop. On the far left is Gov. Charles H. Martin, and standing at right is Gen. George A. White, Oregon's adjutant general. The official party is observing the Grand Review at the 1938 annual encampment.

The 186th Infantry Band gave a concert on Sunday afternoon at the encampment, which drew large crowds from near and far. The bowl-like terrain of Camp Clatsop was one of the best features, in the opinion of staff officers observing the battle demonstrations from the top of the ridge. While the demonstrations went on, the regimental bands played in the background, accompanying the shouts and orders of training men.

Shown here is a demonstration of the .30-caliber Browning M1917 heavy machine gun as part of the famous battle simulations on Grand Review Day at the annual encampments. Crowds numbering over 10,000 would come to witness the display. The 1928 Adjutant General's Biennial Report has a photograph of an Oregon National Guard machine gun squad with this model. It appears that the crowd in the background is all uniformed, including what appears to be men in Navy uniforms.

One account of the demonstration battle described it as follows: "Howitzers belching fire in four-gun salvos; scouts rushing out in trench helmets throwing themselves on the ground, firing live ammunition at targets representing the enemy. Reinforcements arrive in successive waves of riflemen of the 186th to build up the firing line. Following them were the machine guns. Many were massed for a concentration of fire power. Over the crackle of the machine guns [pictured], more howitzers and 37-millimeter guns rained in live ammunition from a far ridge."

In addition to the battle demonstrations, track-and-field competitions were presented for the public to enjoy. The athletic event included a 100-yard dash, a centipede race for eight-man teams, a three-legged race for two-man teams, and a six-man relay. It was one of the distinct pleasures of the commanders and visiting dignitaries to present the medals to the winners. Here, the 100-yard dash is run on the parade grounds around 1935.

More competitions were held away from the public eye. At the obstacle course at Camp Clatsop, many titles were at stake annually. Company L from Astoria held the wall-scaling championship for many years. Here, members of Company L observe their competition, hoping to retain their title one more year.

Back in camp after the competitions, some proud and happy soldiers display their award and pose for a photograph around 1935.

Soldiers of the .30-caliber Browning M1917 heavy machine gun unit relax in the field for a meal, obviously enjoying the sunny weather.

Battery A, 218th Field Artillery performs gun practice on the howitzers. At times before World War II, artillery units occasionally camped and trained at nearby Fort Stevens, as it was thought a more suitable location for such training.

Here is another photograph of field artillery training using howitzers, this time on the beach at Camp Clatsop around 1930.

In this undated photograph, small artillery cannons are being used on the beach at Camp Clatsop. This may be taking place before the days of Camp Clatsop, as the uniforms are pre–World War I. The cannons most closely resemble a Hotchkiss 3.2-inch field gun, but they have not been clearly identified.

Soldiers fire the .30-caliber Model 1903 Springfield rifle at the Camp Clatsop rifle range, using sandbags as prone rifle rests. The Oregon National Guard was equipped with this rifle model from about 1916 to 1940.

This radio set from the early 1930s (SCR-131, 161, or 191) was typically used by infantry troops as a portable, loop, continuous wave (CW) telegraph transmitting and receiving set. The set is designed to give reliable communications between headquarters separated by a distance of five miles or less.

Part of the Quartermaster Corps, these giant Liberty trucks, dating from World War I, were just as imposing and effective for the Oregon National Guard's needs as when they were built. They were considered monuments of motor power for their reliability, although their top speed was about 15 miles per hour. A surviving example of a Liberty truck is in the collection of the Oregon Military Museum.

The logistics and preparation for the training exercises was no small undertaking. Weeks before the arrival of troops, heavy equipment, supplies, and food filled the warehouses at Camp Clatsop. Feeding 3,000 or more troops for two weeks required a minimum of 150 tons of food. In order to convey the necessities of camp, a "deuce and a half" two-and-a-half-ton truck, like the one seen here around 1935, was often employed in long convoys from throughout the state.

Practical needs were often met by local services. Here, an Army truck is refueled by the Associated Oil Company while in the field. Associated Oil may have been contracted to provide such services. It also sponsored radio broadcasts from the post to keep civilian populations apprised of the goings-on at camp.

One of the first buildings to be completed, the quartermaster warehouse still serves the same purpose today. The camp quartermaster was responsible for paying troops at the end of their two weeks at Camp Clatsop. With more than 3,000 troops, the total payroll often exceeded $100,000. The unit commanders received the pay in cash and were responsible for distributing it to individual soldiers. One report estimated additional camp expenses in excess of $45,000.

Contrary to what many believe, it does get dry and dusty on the Oregon coast at times. When such conditions were the case at Camp Clatsop during annual encampments, the water truck was kept busy wetting down the dirt roads throughout post.

Great effort was made to provide entertainment on-post for the men. "Picture shows" were presented every night to large crowds, and the swimming pool, or natatorium, was always popular. Performances and acts from the surrounding communities were also arranged. Sometimes, as here, the men presented the entertainment.

In one interesting anecdote from the mess halls (pictured), complaints had been lodged about the coffee quality at camp in 1938. Maj. Gen. George A. White checked into the matter and promised to "do something about it" if he found the coffee lacking. As a result, all the old-issue coffee was replaced with fresh grounds, and two recipes for correct brewing were distributed to the nearly 50 cooks serving the troops.

Even with all the food that had been trucked in, another item was added to the menu while troops were at Camp Clatsop: razor clams. The abundance of the bivalves on the beach at which the men were training was quickly discovered. The men first tried to use their camp shovels, but the tools proved limited. A great demand for clamming equipment from hardware stores from Seaside to Astoria then arose. Shown here are the Kitchen Police, or "KPs," in 1937.

The log "Chateau," built between 1935 and 1937, was occupied by the commanding officer while at camp. This one of the earliest images of the Chateau, built without dormers, of unpainted exterior logs, and with the exterior window trim painted white. The second chimney extending through the roof is in the kitchen area, and the garage addition is on the north side of the house.

Many miles of fences, similar to snow fences, were built to contain the drifting sand and to allow the grasses to become established. At the same time, shore pines were planted in blocks parallel to and inward from the ocean to stabilize the dunes. These efforts completely stabilized the Clatsop Plains area. Native species are flourishing. It is hard to comprehend how close Oregon came to losing the whole coastal plain from Seaside northward to the Columbia River.

Prior to the military use of the area, development and grazing nearly destroyed nature's ecological balance, and the Clatsop Plains became one vast shifting sand dune with very little vegetation. The dunes seen today are a result of the US Soil Conservation service in the 1930s focusing on the newly developed military training site at Camp Clatsop. The Civilian Conservation Corps performed a massive planting effort with European beach grass in the fore dune area.

This aerial photograph, taken just prior to World War II, illustrates that, by 1941, the post's facilities included the following: 785 floored tent frames; 48 combination kitchens and mess halls; 19 combination shower bath and latrine buildings; 2 headquarters and administration buildings; 2 supply buildings; 2 warehouses; an ordnance repair building; a camp hospital; a natatorium (indoor swimming pool); a camp canteen building; a chapel; a guardhouse; a fully equipped target range; and a combat field firing range.

Two

GENERAL RILEA

Camp Clatsop was renamed Camp Rilea in honor of Maj. Gen. Thomas E. Rilea immediately after Rilea's death on February 3, 1959, in Salem, Oregon. In this wonderful oil painting, Brig. Gen. Thomas Rilea is depicted during his service in World War II. It was painted overseas by a local artist and hung in Rilea's home until it was donated to Camp Rilea after his death.

Born on May 5, 1895, in Chicago, Illinois, Thomas E. Rilea (left) moved with his family to Oregon at a young age. He began his service in the Oregon National Guard in 1914 as a bugler in Company B of the old 3rd Oregon Infantry. He served on the Mexican border in 1916. He is shown here in one of his earliest photographs, at the rank of sergeant.

In 1917, Rilea went overseas as regimental sergeant major (pictured). He attained the rank of captain before returning home from France. He was cited by Gen. John Pershing for meritorious service. Following a short period in civilian life after his return from France in 1919, Rilea reentered the National Guard as captain of infantry in 1921 and was detailed on permanent duty in the headquarters, Oregon National Guard. Possessed with outstanding executive and administrative abilities, Rilea was appointed executive officer of the Oregon National Guard, and in 1924, he was promoted to major, infantry. In 1927, he became lieutenant colonel, Adjutant General's Department, and was assigned as adjutant general, 41st Division.

THE

Oregon Guardsman

MORE COMFORTS
AT CAMP

$50,000 Being Spent at
Clatsop and Stevens

Volume XI   SALEM, OREGON, MARCH 15, 1931   Number 3

In the March 15, 1931, *Oregon Guardsman*, it was reported, "General Rilea Confirmed by Senate." It went on to read, "Confirmation by the United States Senate of the appointment by the President of the United States of Thomas E. Rilea to be a Brigadier General of the Line." A general officer "of the line" is an officer commissioned in the permanent grade of general officer, and he maintains that rank regardless of assignment. The *Oregon Guardsman* was published monthly for many years. In an issue dated February 15, 1924 (volume IV, number 2), Capt. Thomas E. Rilea, Infantry, is listed as the editor.

At the time of his promotion, Brigadier General Rilea held the distinction of being the youngest general officer of the line in the National Guard and the US Army. Rilea was unanimously elected president of the National Guard Association of the United States for the 1936 term at its convention at Santa Fe, New Mexico. Rilea was appointed Oregon adjutant general in 1941. He took time out from this job to serve with the 41st Division in World War II, returning to serve as adjutant general until his death in 1959.

Concurrent with America's involvement in World War II, Maj. Gen. Thomas E. Rilea began his tenure as the adjutant general of the Oregon National Guard. He held the post from 1941 to 1959. His commitment to Camp Clatsop during that time resulted in the expansion and improvement of the post's offerings to an ever-increasing array of groups well beyond the military.

This 1938 gathering of generals involved planning regional troop training maneuvers on the brink of World War II. Shown here are, from left to right, (first row) unidentified; Maj. Gen. George A. White, Salem, commander, 41st Division; (second row) Brig. Gen. Thomas E. Rilea, Salem, commanding, 82nd Brigade; Brig. Gen. Carlos Penington, Tacoma, commander, 81st Brigade; Brig. Gen. Albert H. Beebe, Seattle, commanding, 66th Field Artillery Brigade; Brig. Gen. George C. Marshall, commander, 5th Brigade, Vancouver Barracks (later chief of staff of the Army, promoted to four-star general); unidentified; and Brig. Gen. Maurice Thompson, Washington.

First Lady Eleanor Roosevelt visited American troops based in camps, hostels, and hospitals in Australia in September 1943 as a representative of the American Red Cross. Here, Brig. Gen. Thomas Rilea greets her upon arrival.

In the summer of 1944, Bob Hope hopped from island to island in the South Pacific to entertain the troops. It was an emotional and dangerous journey for Hope and his colleagues. They logged over 30,000 miles and gave more than 150 performances. Shown here are, from left to right, singer Frances Langford, writer Barney Dean, comic Jerry Colonna, guitarist Tony Romano, Hope, dancer Patty Thomas, and Brig. Gen. Thomas E. Rilea.

Seen here soon after his return from his service in World War II, Brigadier General Rilea poses for a new staff photograph as he resumes his duties as adjutant general of the Oregon National Guard. Acting adjutants general filled the office while Brigadier General Rilea served overseas during World War II.

Brigadier General Rilea and his wife, Helen, stand outside of the Chateau in Camp Clatsop in this undated photograph. This and the following two photographs were taken by family members during a summer stay at Camp Clatsop. The family loved the Chateau and spent many happy times on the property.

Taken by the Rilea family, this photograph shows the Chateau in the late 1940s to early 1950s, when the exterior was painted white. The Rileas enjoyed their time on the Oregon coast and at Camp Clatsop. Brigadier General Rilea and his wife, Helen, were both involved in civic organizations and supported events while in the area.

This is a rare interior photograph of the Chateau, taken by Rilea family members. It is said that many of the interior furnishings were acquired when the Lewis & Clark Railroad had a surplus sale. Specifically, there remains a piano on the property from the railroad line. Note the Sunset Brigade insignia over the fireplace. Its current whereabouts are unknown.

Brig. Gen. Thomas Rilea (second from right) and his wife, Helen (far left), pose at a celebration of the Astoria Regatta in the early 1950s. It is apparent that the Rileas enjoyed the coastal communities that had been a part of his military career for so many years via his service in the Oregon National Guard and at Camp Clatsop.

While still serving as adjutant general of the Oregon National Guard, Thomas Rilea died. He was immediately heralded for his lifetime of service to the citizens of Oregon and the nation. When it was announced that Camp Clatsop was to be renamed Camp Rilea, it was reported the name change had long been advocated by Guardsmen, historical groups, and others in the area and supported editorially by the local newspaper. The main reasons for the suggested name change were that it would be an appropriate honor for General Rilea, whose career had involved Oregon National Guard service, and that there had often been great confusion between Fort Clatsop and Camp Clatsop. In the next chapter, the post will be referred to as Camp Rilea to minimize confusion during the transition period following Brigadier General Rilea's death.

Three

THE WAR YEARS

A quintessential Army jeep leaves beachfront patrol or training at Camp Rilea. The three miles of Pacific Ocean frontage allowed for many added training opportunities since the earliest days at Camp Rilea. The vehicle pictured here is actually a one-quarter-ton four-by-four M151 Military Utility Tactical Truck. It is one of the last versions commonly called a "jeep," as a derivation of the original name, "Vehicle General Purpose" or "GP."

Under the National Guard Mobilization Act of 1933, the president could order the troops into federal service if Congress declared a national emergency. Once the Guard was ordered to federal service, World War II brought many changes to the use of Camp Clatsop. It was a primary training and mobilization site for Oregon National Guard units who served throughout the Southwest Pacific region. Astoria's own Company L mobilized from Camp Clatsop for its duty in New Guinea.

Called to active duty for one year of training on September 17, 1940, most Oregon National Guard soldiers did not return until 1945, and some never returned at all. Astoria's Company L, 186th Infantry established a distinguished record in the New Guinea campaign, with combat action in Sanananda, Hollandia, Biak, and in the Philippines at Palawan and Zamboanga. Pictured here in Australia in 1942 are, from Company L, Art Koski (left), Jim Hope (center), and Everett Salvon (killed in Biak).

Since the beginning of Camp Rilea, there has always been a resident engineering company. Here, a proud member of Company C, 162nd Engineer Battalion stands by its encampment at annual training in the late 1940s or early 1950s.

Lined up outside the Orderly Room for Company C, the troops take care of any administrative or pay issues they encounter. The first sergeant (center) appears to be counting out money to the waiting soldier in this photograph from the early 1940s.

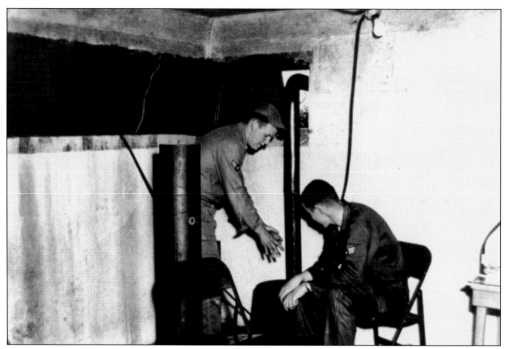

By 1941, Camp Clatsop included over 700 acres and boasted accommodations for 4,600 troops in four-man and eight-man tent frames. Later, these tents were improved by adding wooden walls, metal roofs, and oil-fired stoves, as shown here.

Apparently, it was very exciting and newsworthy when Camp Rilea had new latrines and bathhouses built, as shown in this undated photograph.

The two-and-a-half-ton M135 cargo truck, or "Deuce-and-a-half," was considered the workhorse of the Army. For more than 60 years, these trucks met much of the Army's needs for basic cargo handling and troop transportation. The M135 usually came with a soft-top cab and a canvas-covered metal cargo type body, as pictured here during 1960s-era training at Camp Rilea.

Following World War II, Camp Rilea returned to state control, and it hosted its first postwar encampment in 1948. This era signaled a return to its use as a training facility and also saw an expansion in use from other states around the nation, including Washington, Nevada, Delaware, and Pennsylvania. This trend was to expand and gain momentum as Camp Rilea's reputation as a top-tier location spread among the services.

"Morphine to Mabel, come in Mabel," was what this young girl heard as she and her family ended up in the middle of troop maneuvers at Camp Rilea in late June 1948. The family was on their annual camping trip, and the soldier decided their trailer could serve as the medical tent, protected from aggression. Barely emerging from World War II and on the eve of the Korean Conflict, this experience was one she would never forget. (Courtesy of Mary Strachan Scriver.)

While on their family camping trip, the father had the notion to snap these photographs of the soldiers fully engaged in their field training, emerging from the dunes in June 1948. (Courtesy of Mary Strachan Scriver.)

In 1940, more expansion was under way, including regimental warehouses, kitchens, mess halls, battalion bathhouses and latrines, 650 tent floors, and 5,600 feet of water mains. Materials were supplied by the National Guard, and most of the labor was from the Works Progress Administration (WPA). While these critical infrastructure upgrades were happening, the post was also expanding its area by some 350 acres to accommodate expanded training opportunities. This aerial photograph of Camp Rilea from the south was taken right after World War II.

The US Army developed and fielded the 75-milimeter Skysweeper anti-aircraft weapons system in the early 1950s. It was the first fully integrated weapons system with radar, computer, and gun on one carriage. Here, Battery B, 3rd Gun Battalion, 249th Air Defense Artillery trains on the Skysweeper at Camp Rilea around 1960.

In this photograph, taken around 1959, the 75-millimeter Skysweeper guns of Albany's Battery C, 3rd Gun Battalion, 249th Artillery (AD) prepare for firing at Camp Rilea during the battalion's annual two-week field training. More than 10,000 rounds of ammunition were fired by the Army air defense units during the two-week camp.

In the 1950s, the Army equipped eight battalions with Skysweepers. A number of them were used during the Korean Conflict. Note the decal below the radar disk on this unit preparing to fire at Camp Rilea during training. It depicts a witch flying on a broom, a "skysweeper."

Here, the Oregon Army National Guard M42 Duster is engaging an Army Radio-Controlled Aerial Target (ARCAT) at Camp Rilea about 1960. The ARCAT, referred to as a "drone" aircraft, was used as a target by anti-aircraft units training at the post using many different battle scenarios.

The M42 Duster was a self-propelled anti-aircraft defense weapons system. Twin 40-millimeter Bofors guns were mounted in an open-rotating turret, clearly visible here. This M42 Duster and crew are at the annual training of the 722nd Anti-Aircraft Artillery Battalion, Oregon Army National Guard, at Camp Rilea around 1959.

Although the Army designed the M42 Duster as an air-defense weapon based on the Korean War experience, it played a key role in Vietnam against ground targets. Air-defense units, like the 722nd Anti-Aircraft Artillery Battalion (shown here in 1959), trained on this weapon system at Camp Rilea from 1959 to 1971.

In the mid-1930s, radio-controlled model airplanes became the basis for Army Air Corps development of aerial targets for anti-aircraft gunnery training. Here, the 249th Air Defense Artillery is launching an ARCAT at Camp Rilea in 1961. An ARCAT could be launched from a catapult, a runway (using a three-wheel dolly), or from an airplane. Slusher Lake is in the background.

Radioplane Company of California developed several variations of an original design by former movie star and airplane modeler Reginald Denny. The OQ-19D model ARCAT, shown here being readied for action at Camp Rilea (Clatsop) in 1952, started with battery power.

This OQ-19 ARCAT is having its wing attached at Camp Rilea in 1952. Radioplane started developing this model in 1945, and it was first tested in 1946. About 10,000 of these were built between 1955 and 1958. In this and the next photograph, the row of hutments from the early days of Camp Clatsop are visible.

The 224th ARCAT Detachment of the Oregon Army National Guard operated and maintained ARCATs for anti-aircraft artillery training. Here, troops from the 224th adjust the radio in an ARCAT in 1952. In that same year, Radioplane became a division of Northrop Aircraft Company.

William "Bill" Silas Lane (1935–2004) served in the National Guard for more than 44 years, retiring as the command sergeant major at Camp Rilea in 1995. During his career in the Oregon National Guard, he documented many of the activities of Company M, 186th Infantry and Company E, 162nd Engineers of Tillamook, Oregon. His scrapbook was donated by his family to Camp Rilea after his death. A group of those photographs follows, beginning here, showing Pfc. John House (left) and Lt. Bill Conger of Company M, Tillamook, in 1952. (Photograph by Bill Lane; courtesy of Camp Rilea Archives.)

The M19 60-millimeter light mortar was introduced in 1942. Beyond its lethal purposes, it was also used to light up a battlefield or to provide protective cover for Allied movements during World War II. This mortar also saw action in the Korean and Vietnam Conflicts. In this Bill Lane photograph, a soldier sights a mortar during training at Camp Rilea in 1952. (Photograph by Bill Lane; courtesy of Camp Rilea Archives.)

Pfc. Kenny Dillard sights the mortar at Camp Rilea in 1952. Standing by, in the foreground, is Pfc. Everett Krostag. The men in the back are, from left to right, Cpl. Dean Stephens, Pvt. Henry Veldhuisen, and Cpl. Charles Stephens. As part of the mortar system's design, to keep it lightweight, a spade baseplate was fitted as part of the mount, allowing the crew freedom when dealing with elevation and difficult angles. (Photograph by Bill Lane; courtesy of Camp Rilea Archives.)

This training exercise at Kiwanilong Girl Scout Camp in Warrenton provided excellent engineering training for the troops and doubled as a useful community-service project. Pictured here are, from left to right, Lt. Col. Richard Johannsen, battalion commander; 1st Lt. Henry Callister, commander, Company E, Tillamook; 1st Lt. William Anderson, commander, Company C, Camp Rilea; 2nd Lt. Robert Fastabend, Company C; 2nd Lt. Ray Ward, Company C; and 1st Sgt. Randal Witt, Company E. (Photograph by Bill Lane; courtesy of Camp Rilea Archives.)

National Guard equipment works on a dike across the north end of Long Lake, part of the improvement project undertaken by two engineer companies at the Clatsop Girl Scout Camp (now known as Camp Kiwanilong). Members of Company E, 162nd Battalion, Tillamook, and Company C, 162nd Battalion, Camp Rilea, numbering over 100, bulldozed trails, moved 600 yards of sand for a dike, and cut down or blasted trees obstructing the lake. (Photograph by Bill Lane; courtesy of Camp Rilea Archives.)

Participating in a rope bridge class at Camp Rilea in 1974 are Sp4c. Garry Strange (left) and Specialist Trelstad on the rope bridge. Visible in the background are, from left to right, Sp4c. Pat Murders; Sp4c. Steve Carr, Sp4c. Steve Yates, S. Sgt. Jerry Sutherland, and Specialist Clair. (Photograph by Bill Lane; courtesy of Camp Rilea Archives.)

Sgt. Darren C. Folkers, a member of the 162nd Engineer Company, Tillamook, cuts the tops off fence posts on a newly constructed double apron fence. The fence is to be used in a field training exercise at Camp Rilea. (Photograph by Bill Lane; courtesy of Camp Rilea Archives.)

Seen here in a rigging class in 1974 is Sp4c. David Frampton. He is using a tramway built over Neacoxie Creek for river-crossing training at Camp Rilea. (Photograph by Bill Lane; courtesy of Camp Rilea Archives.)

This 1974 rigging exercise at Camp Rilea involved lifting a jeep. (Photograph by Bill Lane; courtesy of Camp Rilea Archives.)

Sgt. Darren Folkers (right of center) and Spc. Steve Carr (far right) are seen at the demolition site on the extended training areas of Camp Rilea in July 1974. Demolition class was conducted using large stumps left on forestland specifically for this training purpose. (Photograph by Bill Lane; courtesy of Camp Rilea Archives.)

Members of Company E, 162nd Engineers, Tillamook practice building floating bridges at Camp Rilea in August 1962. The ability to assemble a bridge was valuable in wartime, but the Tillamook engineers had plenty of opportunities to employ their training locally when floodwaters threatened. (Photograph by Bill Lane; courtesy of Camp Rilea Archives.)

This aerial photograph was taken in 1961 from the northern end of Camp Rilea. The Chateau can be seen at the bottom, still retaining its garage, which no longer exists.

Four

CAMP RILEA EVOLVES

Maj. Gen. Raymond F. "Fred" Rees holds the distinction of being the only adjutant general to be appointed three times by three different governors. He served four terms as adjutant general for the Oregon National Guard from 1986 until his retirement in 2013 rotating between assignments at the National Guard Bureau in Washington, DC. Simultaneously respected and beloved, Major General Rees was a driving force in over $67 million in improvements and expansion occurring at Camp Rilea during his leadership of the Oregon National Guard. In 2014, he was appointed deputy assistant secretary of the Army for training, readiness, and mobilization at the National Guard Bureau in Washington, DC. When in Oregon, he lives at his ranch near Helix with his wife, Mary Len. (Photograph PC-193191, 24 May 1999, Scott Davis, US Army Information Center, Washington, DC.)

Just prior to the tenures of Maj. Gen. Raymond Rees as Oregon's adjutant general, some revitalization efforts had begun at Camp Rilea. After being reclassified as a Multi-Service Training Installation in 1975, more investment began and updates to facilities were planned. (Author photograph.)

Revamping the front gate was a first step to welcoming new units and organizations training at Camp Rilea. Between 1980 and 1985, a new vehicle-storage building, range-support building, greenhouse, obstacle course, explosives training area, hand-grenade qualification course, and several other projects were completed. (Photograph by Ronald D. Kinsley.)

It was around 1980 that Camp Rilea became an officer's command. Until this point, the post was run by full-time state employees, and unit commanders assumed command when on post. As the sign reads, Col. Richard M. Rusch was the post commander. He was the second commander of Camp Rilea. (Photograph by Ronald D. Kinsley.)

The Oregon National Guard Armory at Camp Rilea was built in 1980. It sits atop the hill just inside the post, to the right after entering the front gate. (Author photograph.)

This memorial garden just inside the front gate, next to the quartermaster building, is just one of the installations around Camp Rilea that was part of the World War II Commemorative Community program. Most of the monuments around the post, including this one, were executed by Astoria Granite Works. (Author photograph.)

Maj. Gen. Raymond F. Rees (right) congratulates Lt. Col. Ronald D. Kinsley at a change-of-command ceremony. The two dedicated citizen soldiers served and worked together over the course of their careers in the Oregon Army National Guard. Their partnership and vision saw over $67 million in improvements at Camp Rilea between 1988 and 2011. Mr. Kinsley (as he was known after his retirement from the Oregon National Guard in 1988) transitioned to facilities manager at Camp Rilea until he retired, again, in 2010.

A permanent home for the full-time caretaker of Camp Clatsop was built in 1931. A.J. Tittenger and his family were the first to move into the "modern, four room cottage," as described in the local newspaper, the *Astoria-Budget*. The lack of a permanent home for the caretaker had been an issue since the opening of the post, contributing to constant turnover in the job. The building is currently unoccupied, but it has provided comfortable housing for many years. (Author photograph.)

Although the M114 carrier pictured here was never used by the Oregon Army National Guard or at Camp Rilea, it is among the military displays placed around today's post to commemorate many eras of armament used in the nation's defense. Designed for command and reconnaissance, the M114 carrier saw extensive service with armored cavalry units during the Vietnam War. (Photograph by Ronald D. Kinsley.)

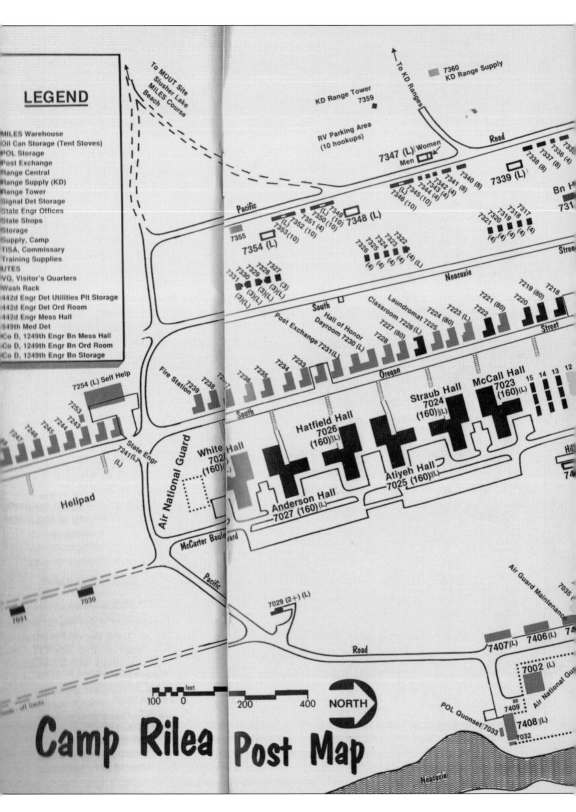

LEGEND

MILES Warehouse
Oil Can Storage (Tent Stoves)
POL Storage
Post Exchange
Range Central
Range Supply (KD)
Range Tower
Signal Det Storage
State Engr Offices
State Shops
Storage
Supply, Camp
TISA, Commissary
Training Supplies
UTES
VQ, Visitor's Quarters
Wash Rack
442d Engr Det Utilities Plt Storage
442d Engr Det Ord Room
442d Engr Mess Hall
549th Med Det
Co D, 1249th Engr Bn Mess Hall
Co D, 1249th Engr Bn Ord Room
Co D, 1249th Engr Bn Storage

To MOUT Site
Slusher Lake
MILES Course
Beach

7360
KD Range Supply

To KD Ranges

KD Range Tower
7359

RV Parking Area
(10 hookups)

Road

7347 (L) Women
Men

7339 (L)

7340 (8)

7341 (8)
7342 (8)
7343 (4)
7344 (4)
7345 (10)
7346 (10)

7338 (8)
7337 (8)
7336 (4)

Bn H
731

7317
7319
7318
7320
7321

Pacific

7349
7350 (10)
7351 (4)
7352 (10)
7353 (10)

7348 (L)

7355

7354 (L)

Neacoxie

Street

7322
7323
7324
7325
7326

7327
7328
7329
7330
7331

Laundromat
7225

Classroom 7226 (L)
7224 (80)
7223 (80)
7227 (80)
7222
7228

7221 (80)
7220

7219 (80)
7218

South
Hall of Honor
Dayroom 7230

Post Exchange 7231 (L)

Street

7233

7236
7235
7234

Fire Station
7239
7238
7237

Oregon

Straub Hall
7024
(160)(L)

McCall Hall
7023
(160)(L)

15 14 13 12

7254 (L) Self Help

7253

7246
7245
7244
7243

South

Hatfield Hall
7026
(160)(L)

Atiyeh Hall
7025 (160)(L)

Hil
74

State Engr
7241(L)
(L)

Air National Guard

White Hall
702
(160)(L)

Anderson Hall
7027 (160)(L)

Helipad

McCarter Boulevard

Pacific

7030

7031

7029 (2+) (L)

Air Guard Maintenance
7035

7407(L) 7406 (L) 74

Road

7002 (L)

Air National Gu

POL Quonset 7033

7409

7408(L)

7032

feet
100 0   200   400

NORTH

Neacoxie

Camp Rilea Post Map

70

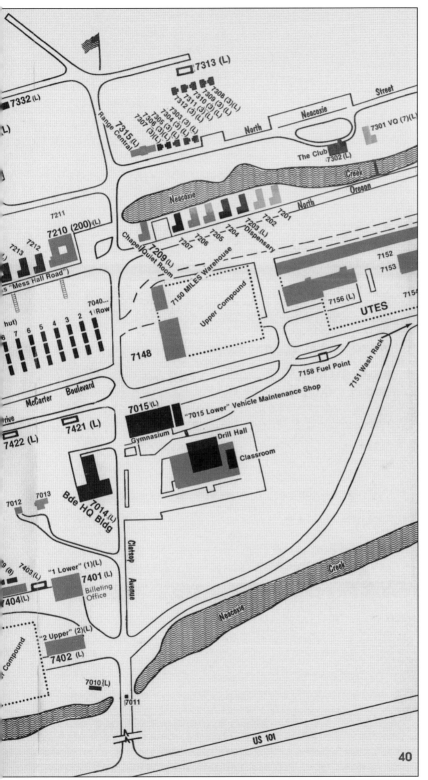

7313 (L)

7332 (L)

7308 (3)(L)
7309 (3)(L)
7311 (3)(L)
7310 (3)(L)
7312 (3)(L)
7303 (3) (L)
7305 (3) (L)
7304 (3) (L)
7306 (3)(L)
7307 (3)(L)

Range Central

7315 (L)

Street

Neacoxie

North

The Club

7301 VQ (7)(L)

7302 (L)

Creek

Oregon

Neacoxie

North

7201

7202

7203 (L)
Dispensary

7204

7205

7206

7207

Chapel/Quiet Room

7211

7210 (200)(L)

7213

7212

7209 (L)

7150 MILES Warehouse

Upper Compound

7152

7153

7156 (L)

7154

UTES

s "Mess Hall Road"

7040...
1 Row

7148

7158 Fuel Point

7151 Wash Rack

hut)

8 7 6 5 4 3 2 1 Row

McCarter   Boulevard

7015 (L)

"7015 Lower" Vehicle Maintenance Shop

rive

7421 (L)

Gymnasium

Drill Hall

7422 (L)

Classroom

7012

7013

Bde HQ Bldg

7014 (L)

Clatsop   Avenue

Creek

9 (8)

7403 (L)

"1 Lower" (1)(L)

7401 (L)

404 (L)

Billeting Office

Neacoxie

Compound

"2 Upper" (2)(L)

7402 (L)

7010 (L)

7011

US 101

40

This map was produced around 1977, prior to the many changes that were about to get under way at Camp Rilea. It can be used as a reference when looking at images depicting the addition of new facilities or the demolition of old structures. The diagram, depicting a post in transition, signals the renewed effort to entice more training to relocate and resume at Camp Rilea. This map was the centerpiece of a professionally produced, 42-page, vest-pocket-sized brochure highlighting all aspects of the post and the surrounding area.

The photographs on this and the following page tell the story of an ongoing process to modernize Camp Rilea. This photograph shows the nearly mile-long row of "hutments," set for demolition. Some do remain, and they have been repurposed for various offices and work spaces. (Photograph by Ronald D. Kinsley.)

This is a closer view of the deteriorating World War II–era wooden buildings set for demolition. It was far more cost-effective to tear down and rebuild facilities designed for the present and future needs of the military than to refurbish all of the wooden structures. (Photograph by Ronald D. Kinsley.)

This scene was replayed throughout Camp Rilea for a decade or more. The demolition was under way. (Photograph by Ronald D. Kinsley.)

As part of the demolition process, and to offer training opportunities, local fire departments participated after the teardowns, performing controlled burns of the remaining materials after any reclamation had been completed. (Photograph by Ronald D. Kinsley.)

The original rappel tower was built in the early 1970s, using troop labor by the construction engineers on post. It was an integral part of the training offerings at Camp Rilea. The tower was replaced in 2009. (Photograph by Ronald D. Kinsley.)

After the initial "take down" of the old rappel tower, Camp Rilea personnel and crew gather for a photograph. Shown are, from left to right, First Sergeant Dintleman, unidentified, Staff Sergeant Mintz, Paul Roehr, Sergeant First Class Lingfelter, Sergeant Campbell, Captain Lyda, Specialist Jones, unidentified, Sergeant First Class Helegso, Sergeant First Class Pond, and Sergeant Staub. (Photograph Ronald D. Kinsley.)

Demolition of the old rappel tower continued with the help of the engineers using a D7G bulldozer. This "Dozer" is one of the workhorses of the construction engineers' equipment inventory and is counted on in many different kinds of projects. (Photograph by Ronald D. Kinsley.)

This aerial photograph was taken about 1995, soon after the battalion headquarters building was completed (slightly right of center) and some of the old buildings had been cleared. Slusher Lake and the Pacific Ocean are in the distance.

In 1994, the Department of Defense World War II Commemoration Committee designated Rilea Armed Forces Training Center as a Commemorative Community, in support for the 50th anniversary of World War II. Deborah Lee, assistant secretary of defense, Reserve Affairs, presented the commemorative community flag to the command of Rilea Armed Forces Training Center on her visit to the post in July 1994. (Photograph by Ronald D. Kinsley.)

Brig. Gen. James Thayer (Ret.), civilian aide to the secretary of the Army, spearheaded the effort for Camp Rilea to become a part of the World War II Commemorative Community program and filed the application. Here, Thayer (left) and Sen. Mark O. Hatfield pose in front of the hand-carved sign announcing Camp Rilea's designation. This sign, along with many other hand-carved signs and pieces around Camp Rilea, were created by Ronald D. Kinsley. (Photograph by Ronald D. Kinsley.)

A key piece of the expansion at Camp Rilea, Sen. Mark Hatfield (pictured) and Maj. Gen. Raymond F. Rees dedicated Koski Hall, the Base Officer Quarters/Base Enlisted Quarters (BOQ/BEQ) building honoring a World War II Silver Star winner from Astoria, William Arthur "Art" Koski. Raised and educated in Astoria, Koski enlisted in the National Guard while in high school. His unit, L Company, was activated for World War II as part of the 41st Infantry Division in 1940. From 1940 to 1945, Koski was in the battles of the South Pacific, including leading his unit in the liberation of Manila in the Philippines. It was here that he was awarded the Bronze and Silver Star medals. (Photograph by Ronald D. Kinsley.)

Maj. Gen. Raymond F. Rees, adjutant general of Oregon, dedicated building No. 7021 as a fitting tribute to the men of L Company, 186th Infantry, memorializing their contributions and sacrifices in World War II. Company L was organized and federally recognized at Astoria as Company G, 186th Infantry, on July 4, 1924, and was redesignated Company L on July 1, 1926. The members shown here are, from left to right, Ted Meredith, Bud Lewis, Maj. James Hope, Capt. John McLoughlin, Ross Peterson, Truman Slotte, Joseph Bruce, Harold Johnson, Col. Warren Lovell, Col. Christian Heid, Lt. Col. Thomas Lattanzi, Alfred Graichen, Lt. Alvin Nicholson, Faville Rickey, Robers Uhrbrand, and Oregon National Guard adjutant general Maj. Gen. Raymond F. Rees. (Photograph by Ronald D. Kinsley.)

Shown here is the obstacle course that had served soldiers well since the 1970s. It was in need of repair and expansion.

In 1993, a new Army-standard confidence course was built, offering 27 different challenges. This updated and nationally rated course has been responsible for bringing many more training groups to Camp Rilea. (Photograph by Ronald D. Kinsley.)

The post headquarters building is pictured here on a sunny day. The flags flying indicate the presence on post of a two-star general (major general). (Photograph by Ronald D. Kinsley.)

Camp Rilea hosts a Veteran's Administration Clinic on post. The clinic offers primary care, laboratory services, and mental health services. When the facility was completed, it eliminated the need of many local veterans to drive to Tacoma or Portland for services. (Author photograph.)

Warrior Hall was built in 2003. Its first use was as a state-of-the-art simulation center, offering the ability to conduct international strategic battle-simulation training. Until the Iraq and Afghanistan conflicts, these training simulations were conducted regularly, but that use has dissipated. Warrior Hall serves as a conference, meeting, presentation, and event space for many military functions and for other organizations. It also houses the new Clatsop County Emergency Operations Center. (Photograph by Ronald D. Kinsley.)

In 1985, six new 160-person barracks buildings were completed. The buildings, called "Starships," were named for past Oregon governors: McCall Hall, Straub Hall, Atiyeh Hall, Hatfield Hall, Anderson Hall, and White Hall. This aerial photograph shows the buildings' central location and ample parking.

As a point of comparison with the previous photograph, this older aerial photograph shows the former buildings in the space where the Starships were built in 1985.

On September 12, 2001, this is what the front gate at Camp Rilea looked like. It was heavily fortified, like every other military installation across the country following the terrorist attacks on the East Coast on September 11. (Photograph by Ronald D. Kinsley.)

Just like every other property on the north Oregon coast, Camp Rilea sustained significant damage during the December 2007 storm that devastated the area. One example was the front gate (pictured), which had one of its two brick pillars washed down from wave action in Neacoxie Creek. The brick debris is visible in the foreground. (Photograph by Ronald D. Kinsley.)

Many repeat visitors to Camp Rilea will recognize the friendly face of the gate guard, Richard Hillgaertner. He is an employee of RAMS Security, the contracted service provider. Using a conservative estimate of 100,000 gate crossings per year, Hillgaertner would have greeted over 1.3 million visitors in his tenure since 2003. He enjoys the work and has a special memory of decorating the guardhouse one year with Christmas lights provided by facilities manager Ronald D. Kinsley. (Author photograph.)

The original construction of the Chapel was completed in 1940. The facility is still functional today, after undergoing upgrades over the years. Services are multidenominational and held on a regular basis. The Chapel is shown here on a rare snow day on the coast. (Photograph by Ronald D. Kinsley.)

A memorial to the late senator and 1930 gubernatorial candidate George Joseph was unveiled at Camp Clatsop on June 16, 1931. It marked the first anniversary of Joseph's death while on a visit to the 1930 Oregon National Guard encampment. Part of the inscription reads: "In Memory of George W. Joseph who died at this spot . . . while observing maneuvers of troops." It is located across the street from the Chapel. (Author photograph.)

Illustrating the many changes that took place between 1985 and 2013, this more recent aerial photograph shows Camp Rilea much as is looks today. Shown here are, from bottom to top through the center of the photograph, the pole yard, 116th Air Control Squadron Headquarters, UTES (Unit Training Equipment Supply) buildings, warehousing, post headquarters, and the Starships. (Photograph by Ronald D. Kinsley.)

Five

A READY FORCE OF CITIZEN SOLDIERS

In the modern era, the evolution of Camp Rilea continues. Since its establishment in 1927, Camp Rilea Armed Forces Training Center has adapted many times to suit the changing training needs of the Oregon National Guard. Today, Camp Rilea is the Oregon National Guard's premier warfighter training center, regional emergency response center, and force projection platform for Oregon soldiers and airmen. It also serves as a world-class center of excellence for installation management, customer service, and community partnering. (Author photograph.)

The 116th Air Control Squadron has called Camp Rilea home since 1988. In 1997, the squadron moved into its new building (pictured) on the north end of Camp Rilea, nearly doubling the space from the old Army barracks on post. The $6.5-million project came into being thanks largely to former senator Mark Hatfield. It is dedicated to the squadron's former commander, the late Col. John G. Nelson, considered a pioneer in the use of radar. (Author photograph.)

Members of the Combat Operations Group of the Oregon Air National Guard assemble for a 2013 group photograph at Camp Rilea. It was the first time the unit's airmen had trained together en masse. Training was held over a five-day period. The Combat Operations Group consists of the 125th Special Tactics Squadron, 116th Air Control Squadron, 270th Air Traffic Control Squadron, and 123rd Weather Flight. (Air National Guard photograph by T.Sgt. John Hughel, 142nd Fighter Wing Public Affairs.)

S.Sgt. Artemio Idelbong and A1c. Summer Cook of the 116th Air Control Squadron, Oregon Air National Guard, train with the latest Air Battle Management equipment in 2011, used in the Middle East on their deployment. The 116th ACS, stationed at Camp Rilea, deployed over 80 airmen as part of its four-month mission to support Operation Enduring Freedom. (Air National Guard photograph by T.Sgt. John Hughel, 142nd Fighter Wing Public Affairs.)

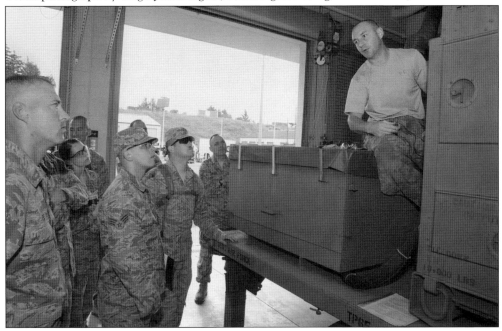

T.Sgt. Richard Lowe (right), 116th Air Control Squadron, Oregon Air National Guard, describes one of the generators the unit maintains to members of the 270th Air Traffic Control Squadron during a joint training session of the Combat Operations Group at Camp Rilea. (Air National Guard photograph by T.Sgt. John Hughel, 142nd Fighter Wing Public Affairs.)

Chief Master Sergeant Bob Birman and his son, S.Sgt. Tyler Birman, both of the 116th Air Control Squadron based at Camp Rilea, deployed to Afghanistan in 2011. More than 80 airmen from the Oregon Air National Guard mobilized for the deployment in support of Air Forces Central Command (CENTAF) and Operation Enduring Freedom.

Airmen of the Oregon Combat Operations Group work together during the "Monster Mash" training exercise, using rafts on Neacoxie Creek at Camp Rilea. Many of the activities were designed to build team cooperation and unit morale. (Air National Guard photograph by T.Sgt. John Hughel, 142nd Fighter Wing Public Affairs.)

Members of the 125th Special Tactics Squadron of the Oregon Air National Guard make their jumps from a CH-47 Chinook helicopter over Camp Rilea in June 2013. (Air National Guard photograph by T.Sgt. Emily Thompson, 142nd Fighter Wing Public Affairs.)

In April 2007, the Oregon Air National Guard welcomed home 28 members of the Camp Rilea–based 116th Air Control Squadron at a demobilization ceremony following their tour of duty at Kandahar Air Base in support of Operation Enduring Freedom in Afghanistan. During its time in country, the 116th ACS controlled more than 39,000 aerial missions. All 28 airmen who mobilized volunteered for the deployment.

In May 2008, the 234th Engineer Company, Oregon Army National Guard, was welcomed home in a demobilization ceremony at the Warrenton High School gymnasium after an eight-month deployment to Iraq. By the end of its mission, the 234th had escorted nearly 6,000 vehicles for 350,000 miles across Iraq; conducted 260 convoys; and maintained the fleet of vehicles. Here, Specialist Isaac and his family enjoy the ceremonies.

Although the in-state mission of the 234th Engineers is to provide crucial vertical construction assets to the Oregon Army National Guard and the state of Oregon, it also undertakes projects benefiting the community. In 1997, the Oregon National Guard unit at Camp Rilea earmarked $112,500 from its federally allocated funds for civilian projects to build a 495-seat stadium for Warrenton High School on the same site as the original field. The bulldozer pictured here is utilized by engineers at Camp Rilea to complete projects. (Photograph by Ronald D. Kinsley.)

A Humvee, or High Mobility Multipurpose Wheeled Vehicle (HMMWV), undergoes maintenance at the Unit Training Equipment Site (UTES) at Camp Rilea. The smaller vehicle in the left foreground, known as a "Gator," is used by Range Control personnel. (Photograph by Ronald D. Kinsley.)

The 234th Engineer Company performs many community-service projects throughout the year. Here, a dozer is removing sand to open the road near the *Peter Iredale* shipwreck at Fort Stevens after a storm. (Photograph by Ronald D. Kinsley.)

An earlier era of the Camp Rilea engineers is represented here by a collection of equipment making up a "Blade Team." This photograph dates from late in the Korean War or early in the Vietnam era. A Blade Team usually consisted of a combination of dump trucks and bulldozers.

Preparing for a year-long deployment to Kuwait, the 234th Engineer Company moves through a mounted training lane during premobilization training at Camp Rilea in May 2014. The soldiers will spend about nine months conducting carpentry, plumbing, and electrical construction missions on US military facilities throughout Kuwait and the surrounding region during the deployment. (Photograph by Sgt. Philip Steiner, 115th Mobile Public Affairs Detachment.)

A great example of a local, state, and federal partnership, the Fort to Sea Trail from Fort Clatsop National Monument to the Pacific Ocean at Sunset Beach runs through and along portions of Camp Rilea. In order to accommodate the project, Camp Rilea modified its water-treatment practices at the time. The new water-treatment facility on post has since eliminated any water treatment near the trail. (Photograph by Ronald D. Kinsley.)

On many occasions, Camp Rilea engineers complete community-service projects during the summer months during Innovative Readiness Training (IRT). This new fishing dock at Slusher Lake on Camp Rilea will be used by children who attend the annual Camp Rosenbaum at-risk youth camp.

Soldiers and airmen from across the country converge at Camp Rilea to compete for the coveted Air Assault and Pathfinder badges. Course instructors travel from Fort Benning, Georgia, as part of the Army National Guard Warrior Training Center's Mobile Training Team. Here, course participants ready their descent from the Sikorsky UH-60 Black Hawk helicopter used in training. (Photograph by Ronald D. Kinsley.)

Camp Rilea received Army certification in 2004 to host the Air Assault courses. Air Assault students are tested on their physical stamina and mental endurance during the grueling physical fitness test, on an obstacle course, and on a 12-mile foot march. A UH-60 Black Hawk hovers at about 70 feet as students rappel as part of the last phase of the training. (Photograph by Ronald D. Kinsley.)

Pathfinder students learn technical skills in planning and executing air movement, air assault, airborne, and air resupply operations. Pathfinders learn to select, mark, and control aircraft landing and pick-up zones, and they acquire air traffic control and navigational expertise. Here, an exercise in airlifting supplies and equipment (known as sling-load operations) is under way. (Photograph by Ronald D. Kinsley.)

During Air Assault, participants learn the basics of missions performed by rotary-wing aircraft. Integral to the curriculum are aircraft familiarization and safety, aero-medical evacuation procedures, ground-to-air communications, and rappelling techniques on both a stationary tower (shown at the Camp Rilea rappel tower) and hovering aircraft. (Photograph by Ronald D. Kinsley.)

These UH-60 Black Hawk mockups were specifically designed for Air Assault School training by Camp Rilea engineers. As part of the dedicated Air Assault Complex, they are used to teach rigging of the UH-60s. The rappel tower and adjacent classroom are nearby. (Photograph by Ronald D. Kinsley.)

These four UH-60 Black Hawks are landing on post for the beginning of the 2014 Air Assault School. In the background, two of the aircraft are coming in for a landing in the "Dig Area" on Camp Rilea. The Dig Area consists of flat, open areas for training with construction equipment like D7 bulldozers, backhoes, and excavators. (Author photograph.)

Citizen soldiers with the Oregon National Guard compete in The Adjutant General marksmanship competition (TAG Match) at Camp Rilea, with the goal to take first-place honors as the Oregon National Guard's top marksman. Annually, more than 50 Oregon National Guardsmen compete against one another with M-4/M-16 rifles, M-9 pistols, Squad Automatic Weapon (SAW) machine guns, .22-caliber pistols, and shotguns. (US Army National Guard photograph by Spc. Erin J. Quirke/Released.)

Even though Camp Rilea has an FAA-designated helipad on post, most incoming helicopters prefer to land on the wide-open parade field. Here, two CH-47 Chinook helicopters stand ready for any of their many uses: troop transport, equipment hauling, or training flights from a regional base. (Photograph by Ronald D. Kinsley.)

The Military Operations in Urban Terrain (MOUT) site is designed for both offensive and defensive squad and platoon-size training. This photograph shows the MOUT's first incarnation in the 1970s. Originally named Millersburg, after the former adjutant general Maj. Gen. Richard A. Miller, the MOUT site can be attacked from land, air, or from the shores of nearby Slusher Lake.

Today's MOUT site is a non-live-fire training facility used to train and sustain combat proficiency in an urban environment. It is used by military and civil police forces for scenario-driven training in law-enforcement and riot-control operations. After the original wooden structures of the MOUT site deteriorated, they were rebuilt (pictured) with materials better able to withstand the coastal climate. The current layout of the MOUT site represents a village in Afghanistan called Khost. (Photograph by Ronald D. Kinsley.)

An interesting training site at Camp Rilea, called a "log crib," is used to practice rope-tying for the Air Assault and Pathfinder classes. It is part of the Air Assault Complex.

This is a great photograph depicting a search-and-rescue (SAR) mission in an urban environment at the MOUT site at Camp Rilea. The soldier has extracted a victim from a smoke-filled building while under fire in this simulation.

Soldiers and airmen from the Oregon National Guard's Counterdrug Support Program train alongside officers from Special Weapons and Tactics (SWAT) units at Camp Rilea. This photograph shows K-9 members of the unit at the MOUT site. The exercise is utilizing the Light Armored Vehicles, or LAVs. Most law-enforcement agencies cannot afford armored vehicles. The Oregon National Guard provides this service and has been involved in hundreds of law-enforcement-related missions. (Photograph by T.Sgt. Nick Choy, Oregon National Guard Public Affairs.)

Completed in 2009–2010, the new rappel tower at Camp Rilea has a 60-foot platform and is the highest in the Army inventory. It has 12 rappel stations, with nine open-face drops and three stations walls. The tower can also be used for fast-rope exercises. Rappel-tower facilities are available to both military and civilian users. (Photograph by Ronald D. Kinsley.)

"Checkpoint Charlie" was built as a training facility for troops during the United States' involvement in the Bosnian conflict. The checkpoint simulated a border crossing and had several sandbag-reinforced bunkers. Designed to be temporary, it no longer exists at Camp Rilea. (Photograph by Ronald D. Kinsley.)

First Sgt. Jeff Dintleman (left) and Camp Rilea's commander, Col. Dean Perez, discuss logistics of the annual Best Warrior Competition held on post. The facilities at Camp Rilea provide the perfect environment, apparatus, and facilities for the various phases of the competition. (Photograph by Lori Tobias.)

The signal that the ranges on Camp Rilea are "hot" is the red flag flying at the post headquarters building and on the range. A "hot" range indicates live fire is being utilized. (Photograph by Ronald D. Kinsley.)

This aerial photograph shows the entire Modified Automatic Record Fire (MARF) Range. The MARF Range is the main live-fire range at Camp Rilea. This range is completely automated and provides the commander and shooters with an accurate score. The beach and the Pacific Ocean are visible in the distance. When there is live fire on the range, troops are posted on the beach to alert beachgoers. (Photograph by Ronald D. Kinsley.)

A soldier is shown in the "fighting position" on the MARF Range. The mounds seen here are automated pop-up targets that are fired upon. Accuracy and scores are recorded by an automated system from a nearby control tower. (Photograph by Ronald D. Kinsley.)

The Machine Gun Transition Range is a four-lane, noncomputerized, manually scored transition range consisting of targets from 100 meters to 500 meters. These soldiers are working on weapons qualifications. (Photograph by Ronald D. Kinsley.)

In the above photograph, soldiers fire their M-4 rifles from the standing position at the MARF Range at a night-fire qualification as part of predeployment training. Camp Rilea has played a role in the training for most Oregon National Guard soldiers deploying to both Afghanistan and Iraq in recent years.

Camp Rilea Unit Training Equipment Site (UTES) is one of two centralized facilities in Oregon providing crew-served weapons and equipment to all military units conducting weekend drills or annual training on the installation. Additionally, the UTES host a covered storage area for military vehicles and seven maintenance bays. By using UTES resources, visiting units can reduce travel time, improve safety and fuel savings, and increase training time and quality. (Author photograph.)

A soldier throws a practice grenade for accuracy and qualification. This range has two lanes on which to qualify soldiers with the employment of hand grenades. This practice range is designed to meet current Army standards.

Camp Rilea has a highly secured ammunition storage facility, ensuring the availability of various types of ammunition for all training purposes. (Photograph by Ronald D. Kinsley.)

This is the control tower for the Modified Automatic Record Fire Range, where all of the firing activities are automated and recorded. The timing of the targets can be programmed according to the user's requirements. (Photograph by Ronald D. Kinsley.)

Unique to Oregon, the Modular Armored Tactical Combat House (MATCH) is a live-fire shoot house. The bi-level, 12-room building allows live fire from 9-millimeter pistol to 5.56-millimeter rifle rounds. It has seven mechanical breech doors on the main level and three upstairs. Each room is equipped with a camera and speakers; all video feeds go to a control room, which can record a training event for use in any after-action review. From the control room, special effects can be introduced to enhance training. (Photograph by Ronald D. Kinsley.)

Carrying an M-4 rifle, a soldier participates in the Best Warrior Competition inside the Modular Armored Tactical Combat House in 2013. His weapon is dummy-corded, indicating no live fire in this scenario.

The Camp Rilea confidence course was built by troop labor and is one of the most used training sites on post. At this facility, individual service members and small teams can confront and overcome various obstacles in order to enhance physical fitness, confidence, and unit cohesion.

Sgt. Ernesto A. Ventura, of the Alaska Army National Guard, descends from Camp Rilea's rappel tower as part of the annual Region VI Best Warrior Competition. (Photograph by Sgt. Betty Boyce, Oregon Army National Guard.)

Shown here is a Multiple Launch Rocket System (MLRS) at a training exercise in the dunes of Camp Rilea. Note the camouflage of the base vehicle.

One of the main features of Camp Rilea is the nearly three miles of Pacific Ocean beachfront. Great effort is made to keep the local communities informed of any training operations taking place on the beach.

US Army specialist Benjamin S. Hermann, with the Oregon Army National Guard's 3670th Maintenance Company, emerges from the beachfront at Camp Rilea after high-crawling approximately 20 yards through the surf while competing in the Region VI Best Warrior Competition. Hermann won the title of Region VI Soldier of the Year, earning the opportunity to compete in the national Best Warrior Competition. (US Army National Guard photograph by Sgt. Betty Boyce/Released.)

Even with all of the advanced weaponry and systems in today's military, every soldier has a story about their "hot dawgs," especially in the infantry. Here, medics apply relief to a soldier's feet while at training at Camp Rilea.

At Camp Rilea, Spc. Donald Snyder is presented with the Oregon National Guard's 2009 Soldier of the Year title by retired Maj. Gen. Curtis Loop (second from left); Brig. Gen. David Enyeart (left), assistant adjutant general of the Army, Oregon; and Oregon State Command Sergeant Major Brunk Conley. Snyder, of Tri-Cities, Washington, is a medic with Detachment 1, 3rd Battalion, 116th Cavalry. In 2012, Command Sergeant Major Conley was selected as the 10th command sergeant major of the Army National Guard at the National Guard Bureau. (Photograph by Sgt. Eric A. Rutherford, Oregon Military Department Public Affairs.)

Six

CAMP RILEA'S VALUED AND EXPANDING PARTNERSHIPS

Appointed adjutant general of the Oregon National Guard in 2013 by Gov. John Kitzhaber, Maj. Gen. Daniel Hokanson graduated from the US Military Academy at West Point in 1986 and served on active duty prior to joining the Oregon National Guard. He has commanded at the company, battalion, and brigade combat team levels, as well as at an Army Aviation Support Facility. General Hokanson is joint-qualified with service on the National Guard Bureau Joint Staff, a forward-deployed Combined Joint Task Force, a Bi-National Command, and Combatant Command. He commanded the 41st Infantry Brigade Combat Team in Iraq and served as chief of staff for Combined Joint Task Force Phoenix in Afghanistan. Together with the dedicated citizen soldiers under his command, General Hokanson's experience and vision will move the Oregon National Guard and Camp Rilea forward into the next era.

Astoria mayor Willis L. Van Dusen (right) greets Maj. Gen. Abdul Wadud, principal staff officer of Armed Forces Division, Bangladesh, during a tour of Camp Rilea. The visit was part of a weeklong tour designed to foster relations between the Oregon National Guard and the Bangladesh military through the State Partnership Program. The program is designed to give operations, logistics, planning, and tactical peacekeeping training in preparation for UN peace-keeping operations. (Courtesy of the *Daily Astorian*.)

Vietnamese military officers toured the region's significant military and cultural presence, including Camp Rilea. The delegation's visit to Oregon is the first of its kind and is the start to a unique military partnership that focuses on emergency-response and disaster-relief training. The delegation spent the day with officers of the Oregon National Guard, touring Camp Rilea, the Astoria Column, the Columbia River Maritime Museum, and Sector Columbia River US Coast Guard Station. (Courtesy of the *Daily Astorian*.)

Maj. Gen. Raymond F. Rees (left), Oregon National Guard adjutant general, and state senator Betsy Johnson congratulates Lt. Col. Dean Perez at a Change of Command ceremony at Camp Rilea in 2012. Upon taking charge of Camp Rilea, Perez became the first local commander of the post. Perez also serves as Clatsop County's emergency management and human resources director. He continues to serve in those roles in addition to his National Guard responsibilities. He was called to active duty twice and served two tours in Afghanistan. (Author photograph.)

Camp Rilea is a training site for SWAT teams from regional law-enforcement organizations. SWAT teams train at different sites throughout Oregon monthly but come to Camp Rilea four times per year to use the facilities. SWAT teams and the Oregon State Police Basic Officer Academy frequently use the ranges for training and weapons qualifications. (Photograph by Ronald D. Kinsley.)

Located adjacent to the 116th Air Control Squadron's facility is the training center for the Northwest Line Joint Apprenticeship Training Committee (JATC). As one of the organization's training facilities across the northwest, Camp Rilea's center is equipped with the latest in power-transmission equipment, such as transformers and switching systems, so that students have hands-on learning that matches actual working situations. (Photograph by Ronald D. Kinsley.)

The Northwest Line JATC was formed in 1957. It provides comprehensive training for experienced line workers who are advancing toward status as outside electrical construction industry journeymen. Students also use a pole yard (pictured) for working simulations of field conditions. All of these training aids replicate the conditions and types of power-transmission devices used in the industry. (Author photograph.)

The Clatsop County Firefighters Association and the Oregon Army National Guard conduct annual fire-training exercises at Camp Rilea. The training event furthers firefighting skills in a prescribed live wildland fire situation using the Incident Command System. This training fosters the cooperative working relationships between Clatsop County Emergency Services, local Structural Fire Departments, and the Oregon Department of Forestry. (Courtesy of the *Daily Astorian*.)

Nearly 100 firefighters participate in the training at Camp Rilea. The Oregon Department of Forestry, along with Astoria, Cannon Beach, Gearhart, Knappa, Lewis and Clark, Olney-Walluski, Seaside, Warrenton, and other rural fire departments partner with the Oregon Military Department and the Oregon State Fire Marshal office in the live-fire exercise. (Courtesy of the *Daily Astorian*.)

Oregon Army National Guard helicopters assist in training from the air utilizing a "Bambi Bucket." This device can carry up to 500 gallons of water and make more than 20 drops before refueling. After scooping up its fill from Slusher Lake, the Bambi Bucket shown here is on its way to help douse the training fire in the dunes of Camp Rilea. The base benefits from hosting this event, because the prescribed fire reduces the threat of range fires.

Camp Rilea takes a great deal of pride in being a vital link to the region's historical and cultural heritage, as well as being a recreational and ecological resource. The post is regularly complimented for its obvious commitment to maintaining the facilities and grounds. (Photograph by Ronald D. Kinsley.)

Brig. Gen. Fred M. Rosenbaum retired in 1986 as assistant adjutant general (Air Force) after a lifetime commitment to the citizens of Oregon in both his military and civilian roles. In 1968, Rosenbaum, a member of both the Housing Authority of Portland (HAP) and the Oregon Air National Guard, came up with the idea of providing a summer experience at Camp Rilea for kids from low-income housing. Initially called HAP Camp, it was renamed Camp Rosenbaum to honor its founder, who passed away in 2010. (Photograph by Ronald D. Kinsley.)

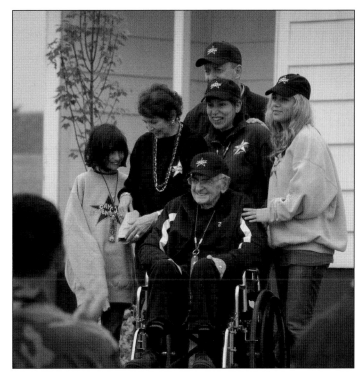

In 2010, Camp Rilea hosted the 40th anniversary of Camp Rosenbaum. Since its inception, Camp Rosenbaum has given nearly 5,000 children a summer camp experience focusing on good citizenship, self-esteem, and strong anti-drug and anti-gang programs. A monument was dedicated to the memory of Brigadier General Rosenbaum at Camp Rilea.

As the signature event of the Astoria Bicentennial Celebration in 2011, country star Reba McIntyre headlined an outdoor concert at Camp Rilea. The more than 6,000 concertgoers enjoyed sunny weather on the same site that many battle demonstrations had been held in Camp Rilea's early days. Also performing were Phil Vassar and the Oregon Army Band. In attendance, enjoying special seating on the stage, were representatives of Walldorf, Germany, who were visiting for

the bicentennial celebration. Many supportive comments were made about the venue, as many attendees had not been familiar with Camp Rilea prior to attending the concert. In 1994, another popular local event, the Crab & Seafood Festival, was held at Camp Rilea. (Courtesy of the *Daily Astorian*.)

Astoria mayor Willis Van Dusen and country star Reba McIntyre lead concertgoers in a rendition of "Happy Birthday" to the City of Astoria in celebration of its bicentennial at the conclusion of the event. (Courtesy of the *Daily Astorian*.)

Many sports camps are hosted at Camp Rilea annually. Football, wrestling, basketball, soccer, and many more public and private sports groups enjoy the convenience of the on-site housing and training facilities. The surrounding area is also a popular spot for families to visit while attending the camps. In this photograph, the Astoria High School football team holds its annual training camp at Camp Rilea. Shown here are coach Howard Rub (left), 2009 AHS graduate Conor Harber (center), and coach Ralph Steinback. (Courtesy of the *Daily Astorian*.)

Another organization with a long history at Camp Rilea is the Boy Scouts of America. For many years, the Columbia Pacific Council has hosted its Cub Scout Day Camp on post.

Three Course Challenge, organized by the Seaside High School track team, was started in 1990 by Neil Branson and Gene Gilbertson. Since then, it has grown into an annual event with over 2,000 participants from schools across the Pacific Northwest and California. It has become one of the largest cross-country meets on the West Coast. Astoria's own Aurora Olson (right) is pictured here participating in the Three Course Challenge. (Courtesy of the *Daily Astorian*.)

What would an Army post be without reenactors? The Pacific Northwest is home to many enthusiastic reenacting groups who frequently take advantage of the opportunity to simulate past battles on the grounds of Camp Rilea. (Photograph by Ronald D. Kinsley.)

On Memorial Day, 2013, Delores Neahring was presented with the Purple Heart and Victory Medal awarded posthumously to her father, Laurence Doten, by Col. Dean Perez, post commander at Camp Rilea. Neahring's daughter Judy Wilson (left) and other family members look on. Many soldiers of Camp Rilea volunteer their time in similar capacities throughout the community by presenting awards, emceeing events, laying wreaths, marching in parades, and participating in other community-service events. (Courtesy of the *Daily Astorian*.)

For anyone with military service, many accommodations are available for rent from post billeting. The "jewel in the crown" is the Chateau. It is said that every Oregon governor since 1927 has stayed at the Chateau except for Barbara Roberts. Meticulously maintained inside and out, the Chateau sleeps 10. Other options are quite comfortable but not as grand. For visitors to Camp Rilea, a drive past this home is a must. (Author photograph.)

From the Chateau to the RV park, Camp Rilea offers a full range of possibilities for travelers to the coast. The RV park has 10 sites, with full hookups, including water, electricity, sewer, and cable. (Author photograph.)

Founded in 1985 and based in Astoria, the Lower Columbia Classics Car Club holds its annual 50s Cruise Reunion at Camp Rilea. (Photograph by Ronald D. Kinsley.)

Camp Rilea is the only Department of Defense installation that boasts a Net Zero water system. The closed-loop system, which effectively takes the water supply off the grid, continually recycles water used on site to preserve local water resources. Although Camp Rilea had been treating and reusing its own water for irrigation since 1978, this enhanced process added a water recycling plant and rapid filtration basins that send treated water back to the aquifer. The achievement has been heralded at all levels of government, and Camp Rilea hosts many dignitaries wishing to learn more. It was completed in 2011 at a cost of $3.2 million. (Author photograph.)

Coexisting with all the activities that take place at Camp Rilea are many forms of wildlife. Roosevelt elk, deer, American bald eagles, Canada geese, waterfowl, and other birds of prey are among the animals to be found. Camp Rilea is considered a game refuge due to its state ownership. Perch, bass, and crappie flourish in all the lakes. Fishing is allowed, but anglers must comply with appropriate state license regulations. (Photograph by Ronald D. Kinsley.)

Since the late 1970s, sixty-eight acres of on-post land was restricted as critical habitat for the threatened Oregon silver spot butterfly under the Endangered Species Act. In recent years, Camp Rilea worked with the North Coast Land Conservancy to preserve appropriate off-post habitat for the threatened species. Other environmental activities at Camp Rilea include dunes restoration programs, a game preserve, tsunami studies, flora and fauna studies, a wastewater treatment facility, and wetlands and watershed studies. Wave and wind energy projects are also being considered for the future.

The new Clatsop County Emergency Operations Center officially opened with a ribbon-cutting ceremony in November 2013. After the December 2007 storm that hit the area, a 2006 agreement with the Oregon Military Department allowing for use of a room at Warrior Hall for emergency operations was deemed inadequate. Plans for a full-scale center were quickly undertaken to enhance regional coordination efforts and response to future emergencies. The installation has its own source of water, can harness power, and has sewer capabilities. Also a tsunami evacuation site, Camp Rilea offers housing facilities for up to 400 in the event of a disaster. (Courtesy of the *Daily Astorian*.)

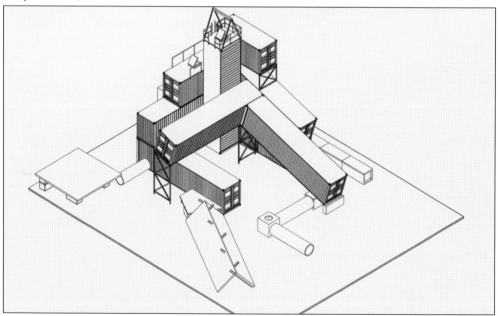

This newly approved project includes the construction and operation of a Structural Collapse Venue Site (SCVS) at Camp Rilea near the existing MOUT site. A priority for the Federal Emergency Management Agency (FEMA) Region 10, it will be used to train first responders in search-and-rescue techniques involving collapsed buildings and structures. There is also a Lifting and Hauling area, consisting of building debris that must be moved and lifted with hand tools, and a Breaching and Breaking area, with building materials that must be cut or broken using hand-carried power tools.

ABOUT THE ORGANIZATIONS

The author has committed to donate her royalties of this book to the Camp Rilea Post Welfare Fund. The money is used to preserve the history of Camp Rilea and for other projects deemed necessary by post management. If you would like to support this, or the following organizations, a donation will be most appreciated.

Camp Rilea Post Welfare Fund
c/o Facilities Manager
Camp Rilea Armed Forces Training Center
33168 Patriot Way
Warrenton, OR 97146
www.camp-rilea.org

Brigadier General James B. Thayer Oregon Military Museum
Camp Withycombe
15300 SE Minuteman Way
Clackamas, OR 97015
Phone 503-683-5359
Fax 503-683-4913
www.oregonmilitarymuseum.org

Daughters of the American Revolution, Astoria Chapter
Attn: Camp Rilea Soldiers Coffee Fund
115 Skyline Avenue
Astoria, OR 97103

DISCOVER THOUSANDS OF LOCAL HISTORY BOOKS
FEATURING MILLIONS OF VINTAGE IMAGES

Arcadia Publishing, the leading local history publisher in the United States, is committed to making history accessible and meaningful through publishing books that celebrate and preserve the heritage of America's people and places.

Find more books like this at
www.arcadiapublishing.com

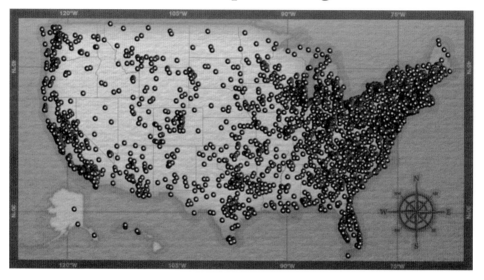

Search for your hometown history, your old stomping grounds, and even your favorite sports team.

MADE IN THE USA